Sheet
Your Ultimate Guide to Sheet Pan Recipes

[MATTHEW LIVINGSTON]

Legal & Disclaimer

The information contained in this book and its contents is not designed to replace or take the place of any form of medical or professional advice; and is not meant to replace the need for independent medical, financial, legal or other professional advice or services, as may be required. The content and information in this book has been provided for educational and entertainment purposes only.

The content and information contained in this book has been compiled from sources deemed reliable, and it is accurate to the best of the Author's knowledge, information and belief. However, the Author cannot guarantee its accuracy and validity and cannot be held liable for any errors and/or omissions. Further, changes are periodically made to this book as and when needed. Where appropriate and/or necessary, you must consult a professional (including but not limited to your doctor, attorney, financial advisor or such other professional advisor) before using any of the suggested remedies, techniques, or information in this book.

Upon using the contents and information contained in this book, you agree to hold harmless the Author from and against any damages, costs, and expenses, including any legal fees potentially resulting from the application of any of the information provided by this book. This disclaimer applies to any loss, damages or injury caused by the use and application, whether directly or indirectly, of any advice or information presented, whether for breach of contract, tort, negligence, personal injury, criminal intent, or under any other cause of action.

You agree to accept all risks of using the information presented inside this book.

You agree that by continuing to read this book, where appropriate and/or necessary, you shall consult a professional (including but not limited to your doctor, attorney, or financial advisor or such other advisor as needed) before using any of the suggested remedies, techniques, or information in this book.

Table of Contents

Introduction

We all have a sheet pan on hand, tucked somewhere beneath the oven or in our pantry, just waiting for us to get out of the fast food joint, get serious about our health, and get roasting and baking. The old days, when our mothers slumped over multiple pots and pans, stirring and steaming and roasting and whatever else, taking the time and effort to build beautiful meals, but subtracting that time from their own lives, are over. Thank goodness.

Luckily for us, living in the future, "sheet pan recipes" are now a thing— allowing us to place many different vegetables and proteins on a single pan and then dive into the glory of a four, six, or eight serving meal. It's about as simple as cooking can get, outside of just going to a restaurant to get a meal.

But losing weight while cooking your own meals can be just as difficult as any other diet plan (after all, dieting is one of the most difficult things in the world), with many people gaining weight when they utilize too many carbohydrates in a single serving. Carbs are not necessarily "the devil," as many people would call them, but they aren't necessarily working with your weight loss plans. Carbohydrates are literally "sugar" after they're broken down in your body, and they disallow your body from using your stored fat cells for energy. Therefore, when you continue to fuel yourself with carbohydrates like breads, pastas, too many potatoes, etc., nothing falls off your thighs or waist. It doesn't have to. Therefore, you have to tweak your diet—with meals that are less than 15 grams of net carbohydrates per serving—to shell off your "winter layer." And fortunately, with this book, you no longer have to pay such special attention.

A low carb diet plan allows you to lose up to two to three times more weight than normal "diet plans," since it works with the scientific mechanisms of your body to shrink your fat cells. For one, when you restrict carbohydrates, you're decreasing your levels of insulin pulsing through your blood. When your insulin levels are too high, this disallows your fat cells to shrink and forces you to store glucose in your cells, rather than use it for fuel. Plus, having too much insulin in your body can promote a whole host of other symptoms, and also lead to diabetes, which makes weight loss even more difficult down the line. As such, a low carb diet is better in both the long and short-term plans, making you thin and beautiful and healthy NOW, as well as later.

Furthermore, most low carb diet plans are very high in protein, which allows you to boost your metabolism, reduce your appetite, and thus help you build muscles which will make you look sleek and thin. Know that if you decrease your carbohydrate levels with this boosted protein levels, you will probably "bulk up," and if you're just looking to reduce, you can't get enough protein. Your body will thank you.

With this cookbook, which outlines your protein count, your fat amount, your net carbohydrates (which is the number of carbohydrates minus the amount of fiber), and your calories, you can keep track of your weight loss goals, drop pounds, and finally fit into your skinny jeans. And you can do that all with a single sheet pan, and with stunning, delicious, and nutritional ingredients.

Breakfast Recipes

Mixed Nut Granola

Serves: 10

Preparation time: 40 minutes

Ingredients:

- 1 cup almonds

- 1 cup hazelnuts

- 1 cup walnuts

- 1 cup flax seeds meal

- ¼ cup cocoa powder

- Salt, to taste

- ¼ cup hazelnut oil

- ¼ cup melted butter

- 2-ounces chopped unsweetened chocolate

- ½ cup swerve (sugar substitute)

Directions:

1. Preheat the oven to 300 degrees F.

2. Line a large rimmed baking sheet with parchment paper.

3. In a food processor, add almonds, hazelnuts and walnuts and pulse till coarse crumb forms.

4. Transfer the nut mixture into a large bowl.

5. Add flax seeds meal, cocoa powder, and salt and mix well.

6. In a pan, add hazelnut oil, butter, and chocolate on low heat.

7. Cook for about 2-3 minutes or till smooth, stirring continuously.

8. Stir in swerve and immediately, remove from heat.

9. Add the butter mixture over nut mixture and toss to coat well.

10. Transfer the mixture onto prepared baking sheet evenly.

11. Bake for about 15 minutes, stirring after every 5 minutes.

12. Turn off the oven but keep the baking sheet in oven for about 20 minutes, stirring occasionally.

Banana Bread

Serves: 12

Preparation time: 1 hour 20 minutes

Ingredients:

- 2 cups all-purpose flour

- 1 teaspoon baking soda

- Salt, to taste

- ¾ cup brown sugar

- ½ cup softened unsalted butter

- 2 eggs, beaten lightly

- 1 teaspoon vanilla extract

- 2 1/3 cups peeled and mashed bananas

- ¼ cups toasted and chopped walnuts

Directions:

1. Preheat the oven to 350 degrees F.

2. Grease a 9x5-inch a bread loaf pan.

3. In a large bowl, mix together flour, baking soda and salt.

4. In another bowl, add brown sugar and butter and beat till creamy.

5. Add the eggs and vanilla extract and beat till well combined.

6. Add bananas and beat till well combined.

7. Add egg mixture into the bowl with flour mixture and mix till just moistened.

8. Gently, fold in walnuts.

9. Place banana slices over mixture in two rows.

10. Transfer the mixture into prepared bread loaf pan evenly.

11. Bake for about 65 minutes or till a toothpick inserted in the center comes out clean.

12. Remove the loaf pan from oven and place on a wire rack to cool for at least 10-15 minutes.

13. Carefully, invert the bread to remove from loaf pan.

14. With a sharp knife, cut the bread loaf in desired size slices.

Lemony Quinoa Bread

Serves: 12

Preparation time: 2 hours

Ingredients:

- 1¾ cups uncooked quinoa (soaked for overnight and rinsed)

- ¼ cup chia seeds (soaked in ½ cup of water for overnight)

- ½ teaspoon bicarbonate soda

- Salt, to taste

- ½ cup of water

- ¼ cup olive oil

- 1 tablespoon fresh lemon juice

Directions:

1. Preheat the oven to 320 degrees F.

2. Line a loaf pan with a parchment paper.

3. In a food processor, add all ingredients and pulse for about 3 minutes.

4. Transfer the mixture into prepared loaf pan evenly.

5. Bake for about 1½ hours.

6. Remove from the oven and keep on wire rack for about 30 minutes before removing from loaf pan.

Blueberry Muffins

Serves: 10

Preparation time: 25 minutes

Ingredients:

- 2½ cups almond flour

- 3 tablespoons ground cinnamon, divided

- ½ teaspoon baking soda

- Salt, to taste

- 2 eggs

- ¼ cup maple syrup

- ¼ cup of coconut milk

- ¼ cup melted coconut oil

- 1 tablespoon coconut flour

- 1 tablespoon vanilla extract

- 1 cup fresh blueberries

Directions:

1. The oven should be preheated to 350 degrees F.

2. Grease 10 cups of a large muffin pan.

3. In a large bowl, mix together flours, 2 tablespoons of cinnamon, baking soda, and salt.

4. In another bowl, add maple syrup, eggs, milk, oil, and vanilla and beat till well combined.

5. Add egg mixture into flour mixture and mix till well combined.

6. Fold in blueberries.

7. Place the mixture into prepared muffin cups evenly and sprinkle with cinnamon.

8. Bake for about 22-25 minutes or till a toothpick inserted in the center comes out clean.

Salmon and Brown Rice Frittata

Serves: 4

Preparation time: 15 minutes

Ingredients

- Olive oil, for greasing the pan

- 1 egg

- 4 egg whites

- ½ teaspoon dried thyme

- ½ cup cooked brown rice

- ½ cup cooked, flaked salmon (about 3 ounces)

- ½ cup fresh baby spinach (see Tip)

- ¼ cup chopped red bell pepper

- 1 tablespoon grated Parmesan cheese

Directions:

1. Rub a 6-by-2-inch pan with a bit of olive oil and set aside.

2. In a small bowl, beat the egg, egg whites, and thyme until well mixed.

3. In the prepared pan, stir together the brown rice, salmon, spinach, and red bell pepper.

4. Pour the egg mixture over the rice mixture and sprinkle with the Parmesan cheese.

5. Bake for about 15 minutes, or until the frittata is puffed and golden brown. Serve.

Sausage Egg Muffins

Serves: 12

Preparation Time: 40 minutes

Ingredients

- 12 oz. cooked sausage crumbles

- 12 eggs

- ¼ cup milk

- 2 cups cheddar cheese, sharp, hand-shredded

- ¼ tablespoon black pepper or chili pepper

Directions

1. Mix all the ingredients.

2. Pour into 12 greased muffin papers (in a pan).

3. Bake at 375 degrees for 29 minutes.

4. Cool for 4 minutes before serving.

Freezing Instructions

5. After cooling, place in baking sheet. For the best flavor, heat in microwave or toaster oven before eating.

Asparagus and Bell Pepper Strata

Serves: 4

Preparation time: 20 minutes

Ingredients

- 8 large asparagus spears, trimmed and cut into 2-inch pieces

- ⅓ cup shredded carrot (see Tip)

- ½ cup chopped red bell pepper

- 2 slices low-sodium whole-wheat bread, cut into ½-inch cubes

- 3 egg whites

- 1 egg

- 3 tablespoons 1 percent milk

- ½ teaspoon dried thyme

Directions:

1. In a 6-by-2-inch pan, combine the asparagus, carrot, red bell pepper, and 1 tablespoon of water. Bake in the air fryer for 3 to 5 minutes, or until crisp-tender. Drain well.

2. Add the bread cubes to the vegetables and gently toss.

3. In a medium bowl, whisk the egg whites, egg, milk, and thyme until frothy.

4. Pour the egg mixture into the pan. Bake for 11 to 15 minutes, or until the strata are slightly puffy and set and the top starts to brown. Serve.

Spinach and Swiss Quiche

Serves: 4

Preparation Time: 48 minutes

Ingredients

- 2 tablespoon butter

- 6 oz. frozen chopped spinach, drained and thawed

- 1 cup cream

- 1 cup hand-shredded swiss cheese or hand-shredded cheese

- ¼ tablespoon salt

- 1 diced white onion

- 4 eggs

- ⅛ tablespoon nutmeg

- ¼ tablespoon black pepper, ground

Directions

1. Heat the oven to 350 degrees.

2. Then spray a pie pan with your choice of cooking spray. Spray liberally as eggs may stick.

3. Cook onions in butter till glassy, then add the spinach and simmer until the water is gone.

4. Mix all of the ingredients in a bowl, including the spices.

5. Pour into the baking sheet.

6. Bake for 29 minutes.

7. Cool for 9 minutes and cut into quarters.

8. Wrap a cooled slice of quiche in saran wrap, then place in a zip-lock bag. Microwave for 1 minute in two 30-second bursts.

Veggie Frittata

Serves: 4

Preparation time: 12 minutes

Ingredients

- ½ cup chopped red bell pepper

- ⅓ cup minced onion

- ⅓ cup grated carrot

- 1 teaspoon olive oil

- 6 egg whites

- 1 egg

- ⅓ cup 2 percent milk

- 1 tablespoon grated Parmesan cheese

Directions:

1. In a 6-by-2-inch pan, stir together the red bell pepper, onion, carrot, and olive oil. Put the pan into the air fryer. Cook for 4 to 6 minutes, shaking the basket once until the vegetables are tender.

2. Meanwhile, in a medium bowl, beat the egg whites, egg, and milk until combined.

3. Pour the egg mixture over the vegetables in the pan. Sprinkle with the Parmesan cheese. Return the pan to the air fryer.

4. Bake for 4 to 6 minutes more, or until the frittata is puffy and set.

5. Cut into 4 wedges and serve.

Almond Bread

Serves: 8

Preparation Time: 25 minutes

Ingredients:

- 2 eggs

- 1 cup almond butter, unsalted

- 3/4 cup almond flour

- 1 Tbsp cinnamon

- 1 tsp pure vanilla extract

- 1/4 tsp baking soda

- 2 Tbsp liquid Stevia

- 1/2 tsp sea salt

Directions:

1. Preheat oven to 340 F degrees.
2. In a deep bowl whisk eggs, almond butter, honey, Stevia, and vanilla. Add in salt, cinnamon, and baking soda. Stir until all ingredients are well combined.
3. Pour dough into a greased baking pan. Bake for 1215 minutes.
4. Once ready, let cool on a wire rack. Slice and serve.

Main Dishes

Easy Sheet Pan Chicken Legs

Serves: 4-6

Preparation time: 20 minutes

Ingredients

- 8-10 chicken legs

- 1 onion, sliced

- ¼ tsp dried thyme

- 2 cubed sweet potatoes, medium-sized

- 2 garlic cloves, sliced

- 1 orange, zested

- 1 tsp sea salt

- Juice of half an orange

- 1 bulb fennel, sliced

- ¼ tsp black pepper

- 2 tbsp. olive oil

- 4 lemon slices for garnish

Directions:

1. First, preheat your oven to 400 degrees Fahrenheit.

2. Next, spread the chicken legs out on a clean sheet pan. Place your vegetables around and between the chicken legs.

3. To the side, using a whisk, mix together the olive oil, orange zest, orange juice, and thyme.

4. Season the chicken legs and vegetables with salt and pepper and pour the mixture over everything.

5. Bake for approximately 45 minutes or until the chicken is no longer pink in the center and the vegetables are soft and golden. Garnish with lemon slices and serve.

Lime and Cilantro Chicken

Serves: 4

Preparation Time: 25 minutes

Ingredients:

- 2 chicken breasts, medium-sized
- 1/3 cup chopped cilantro
- 1 sliced bell pepper
- 3 minced garlic cloves
- Juice from one lime
- 2 tbsp. olive oil
- ½ tsp. paprika
- ½ tsp. cumin
- Salt
- Pepper

Directions:

1. First, preheat your oven to 450 degrees Fahrenheit.

2. Next, to the side, in a large bowl, stir together the cilantro, garlic, lime juice, olive oil, and the paprika and cumin. Add the chicken and the peppers to the bowl, and stir until well combined.

3. Next, place the chicken and vegetables on a large baking sheet, and bake for 20 minutes or until chicken is cooked through. The chicken should be golden-brown, and the peppers should be blackened slightly.

4. Serve warm, and enjoy.

Mediterranean Sheet Pan Chicken and Vegetables

Serves: 4

Preparation Time: 40 minutes of marinating plus 40 minutes of preparation/cook time.

Ingredients:

- 8 ounces skinless and boneless chicken

- 10 ounces diced zucchini

- 2 diced carrots

- 1 diced red bell pepper

- 1 diced onion

- 1 diced yellow bell pepper

- 1 cup chopped parsley

- ½ tsp. onion powder

- ½ tsp. thyme

- ½ tsp. basil

- 1 minced garlic clove

- 2 tbsp. red wine vinegar

- 2 tbsp. olive oil

Directions:

1. First, preheat the oven to 450 degrees Fahrenheit. Place aluminum foil over a sheet pan, and then place the oven rack on the lower third of the oven.

2. Next, stir together the seasonings, oils, and vinegar, including thyme, onion powder, basil, garlic, red wine vinegar, and olive oil in a large bowl.

3. Salt the chicken, and then place the chicken, carrots, zucchini, peppers, and the onion in the large bowl. Toss well to coat the chicken and vegetables with the prepared mixture, and then allow the chicken and vegetables to sit for 40 minutes until marinated.

4. Next, place the ingredients on a baking sheet, in a single layer. The chicken and the vegetables shouldn't touch each other.

5. Bake the ingredients for 20 minutes. After 20 minutes, turn the chicken and the vegetables, and bake for another 10 minutes. Everything should be well roasted and very tender.

6. Add parsley to the mixture, and serve. Enjoy.

Sheet Pan Chicken Fajitas

Serves: 6

Preparation Time: 35 minutes

Ingredients:

- 1 pound chicken, sliced
- 1 diced green pepper
- 1 diced yellow pepper
- 1 diced red pepper
- 2 tsp. chili powder
- ½ tsp. garlic powder
- 1 tsp. cumin
- 1 tsp. salt
- 1 tsp. pepper
- 1/3 cup olive oil

Directions:

1. First, preheat the oven to 400 degrees Fahrenheit.

2. Next, stir together the spices: chili powder, garlic powder, cumin, salt, and pepper. Add the oil, and stir well.

3. Next, toss this mixture with the vegetables and the chicken, and spread out the mixture on a sheet pan.

4. Bake the mixture for 30 minutes, or until the chicken is cooked all the way through and the vegetables are crispy.

5. Serve with your favorite toppings, including avocadoes or sour cream, and enjoy.

Flavorful Mustard Chicken

Serves: 8

Preparation Time: 50 minutes

Ingredients:

- 3 pounds chicken, with bone, and patted dry

- 3 tbsp. mustard, whole-grain

- 3 minced garlic cloves

- 1 tbsp. butter

- 1 tbsp. minced thyme leaves

- 2 tsp. Dijon mustard

- 1 tsp. pepper

- 1 tsp. salt

- olive oil

- ½ cup dried breadcrumbs

Directions:

1. First, preheat the oven to 425 degrees Fahrenheit. To the side, stir together the whole-grain mustard, garlic, thyme, and the Dijon mustard. Add the butter, softened, and stir well.

2. Next, salt and pepper the chicken. Rub the created mixture of butter and spices over the chicken. Add the breadcrumbs in a shallow bowl or a plate, and coat the chicken with the breadcrumbs.

3. Now, place the chicken on a baking sheet. Add a bit of olive oil overtop, in a small drizzle.

4. Next, bake the chicken for 40 minutes. Serve, and enjoy.

Bruschetta Sheet Pan Chicken

Serves: 4

Preparation Time: 40 minutes

Ingredients:

- 4 skinless and boneless chicken breasts

- Salt and freshly ground pepper

- 3 tbsp. olive oil

- 10 ounces halved red potatoes

- 4 minced garlic cloves

- 1 tsp. thyme, dried

- 1/3 cup grated Parmesan

- 4 ounces mozzarella cheese, sliced into 1-ounce pieces

Bruschetta Ingredients:

- 1 tbsp. balsamic vinegar

- 2 ½ cups halved cherry tomatoes

- 2 minced garlic cloves

- 1/3 cup chopped basil leaves

- Salt and pepper to taste

Directions:

1. First, preheat the oven to 400 degrees Fahrenheit.

2. Stir together the bruschetta ingredients, once completely prepared, in a medium-sized bowl. Salt and pepper to taste. Set the mixture to the side.

3. Next, salt and pepper the chicken. Place the chicken on a baking sheet in a single layer, on one half of the baking sheet. Add the red potatoes to the other half of the baking sheet, and then add the garlic, olive oil, thyme, and the Parmesan overtop, tossing to coat. Next, salt and pepper to taste.

4. Place the pan in the oven, and bake for about 25 minutes, until chicken is cooked and the potatoes are golden.

5. Add the mozzarella to the top of the chicken during the very last five minutes of baking.

6. Serve the chicken and potatoes immediately, topped with the bruschetta mixture.

Balsamic Chicken with Green Beans and Tomatoes

Serves: 6

Preparation Time: 70 minutes

Ingredients:

- 2 pounds of chicken breasts

- 3 tbsp. olive oil, divided

- 1/3 cup balsamic vinegar

- 5 tbsp. honey

- 2 minced garlic cloves

- 1 tsp. rosemary, dried

- 1 tsp. dried thyme

- ½ tsp. pepper

- 1 tsp. salt

- 1 pint of cherry tomatoes

- ¾ pound green beans

Directions:

1. First, preheat the oven to 425 degrees Fahrenheit.

2. Next, stir together the honey, vinegar, one of the tbsp. olive oil, thyme, rosemary, garlic, salt, and pepper.

3. Add the chicken to the bowl of the marinade, and allow it to soak for 30 minutes.

4. While the chicken is marinating, place the cherry tomatoes on the sheet pan, drizzle them with the rest of the olive oil, and allow them to bake for 25 minutes.

5. Afterward, add the green beans to the sheet pan.

6. Remove the chicken from the bowl, and place the chicken over the vegetables.

7. Next, pour the rest of the marinade from the bowl, over the chicken and vegetables.

8. Bake the vegetables and chicken for 40 minutes, basting the chicken breasts with the pan's various juices as it cooks.

9. Afterward, allow the chicken to sit for 10 minutes before serving. Serve with the pan juices, oozing over the chicken, and enjoy.

Parmesan, Lemon, and Garlic Chicken

Serves: 4

Preparation Time: 60 minutes

Ingredients:

- 4 boneless and skinless chicken breasts

- 1 egg

- 2 tbsp. lemon juice

- 1 tbsp. chopped parsley

- 3 minced garlic cloves

- ½ cup breadcrumbs

- ½ tsp. salt

- ½ tsp. pepper

- ½ cup grated Parmesan

Directions:

1. First, preheat the oven to 400 degrees Fahrenheit.

2. Next, stir together the egg, garlic, lemon juice, parsley, and some salt and pepper.

3. Dip the chicken pieces into the lemon and egg mixture, covering them in the juices. Allow the chicken to marinate for 30 minutes.

4. Next, to the side, stir together the breadcrumbs with the Parmesan cheese.

5. Remove the chicken from the lemon and egg mixture, and coat them with the breadcrumbs and Parmesan. Place the chicken on a baking sheet, and then bake the chicken for 15 minutes. At this time, flip the chicken breasts, and set the oven to broil.

6. Broil the chicken breasts for 10 minutes, or until the chicken is crispy.

7. Add parsley over the chicken to serve, and enjoy.

Chicken Wrapped With Prosciutto

Serves: 4

Preparation Time: 40 minutes

Ingredients:

- 2 pounds boneless and skinless chicken breasts, sliced into four pieces

- 2 slices of prosciutto for each chicken breast

- 4 tsp. Dijon mustard

- 6 slices of provolone cheese

- ½ pound halved cherry tomatoes

- ¾ pound asparagus, trimmed

- 1 tbsp. red wine vinegar

- 1 tbsp. olive oil

- 2 minced garlic cloves

- ½ tsp. salt

- ½ tsp. pepper

Directions:

1. First, preheat the oven to 425 degrees Fahrenheit. Ensure that the oven rack is in the center of the oven.

2. Next, stir together the minced garlic, vinegar, oil, salt, and the pepper in a medium-sized bowl.

3. Next, salt your chicken breasts. Add 1 tsp. of Dijon mustard to each chicken breast, and then add two slices of Prosciutto to your cutting board or another work surface. Place the cheese in the center of the prosciutto, and then add the chicken, with the

mustard down. Wrap the prosciutto and cheese around the chicken, and then place the wrapped chicken on the sheet pan.

4. Next add the created "marinade" over the trimmed asparagus. Toss to coat the asparagus, and place the asparagus alongside the chicken.

5. Next, add the tomatoes to the marinade bowl, and swirl them to coat them. Place them on the baking sheet.

6. Cook the asparagus, tomatoes, and the chicken in the oven for 30 minutes.

7. Afterwards, remove the chicken, asparagus, and tomatoes from the oven, and enjoy.

Chicken Piccata

Serves: 4

Preparation Time: 20 minutes

Ingredients:

- 4 chicken thighs Dash of salt and black pepper

- 4 tablespoon of extra virgin olive oil

- 6 ounces of butter, soft

- ¼ cup of white wine, dried

- ¼ cup of lemon juice, fresh

- ½ cup of chicken stock

- ¼ cup of capers, brined

- 4 tablespoon of heavy cream

- ¼ cup of parsley, fresh and chopped

Directions:

1. Season the chicken thighs with a dash of salt and black pepper.

2. Place a large baking sheet over medium to high heat. Add in the extra virgin olive oil and two tablespoons of soft butter. Once the butter begins to simmer add in the chicken thighs. Cook for 5 minutes on each side or until cooked through. Remove from the baking sheet and transfer to a large plate.

3. Add the dried white wine into the baking sheet and deglaze the pan.

4. Add in the fresh lemon juice, chicken stock, and capers. Stir well to mix and bring the mixture to a boil. Once boiling reduces the heat to low.

5. Add the chicken back into the baking sheet. Allow simmering for 5 minutes.

6. Transfer the chicken back into a large plate.

7. Add the heavy cream and remaining butter into the baking sheet. Season with a dash of salt and black pepper. Whisk to mix.

8. Pour the sauce over the chicken. Serve with a garnish of parsley.

Turkey with Honey-Roasted Flair

Serves: 8

Preparation Time: 95 minutes

Ingredients:

- 4 pounds of boneless turkey breasts

- 4 sliced carrots

- 7 sprigs of thyme, fresh

- 2 tbsp. honey

- 1 sliced fennel bulb

- 1 sliced sweet potato

- 1 diced onion

- 4 tbsp. butter, melted

- Salt and pepper

Directions:

1. First, preheat the oven to 400 degrees Fahrenheit.

2. Next, rub the salt and pepper outside of the turkey, coating it and rubbing it into every crevice and beneath the skin.

3. Add the honey to the turkey next, coating it well, making sure not to put the honey on top of the turkey skin.

4. Next, to the side, on the baking sheet, stir together the vegetables and the thyme, along with two of the tbsp. of melted butter.

5. Brush the rest of the butter on the turkey.

6. Place the turkey on the pan, and spread the vegetables and turkey evenly.

7. Cook the turkey and vegetables for 15 minutes, then reduce the temperature to 325 degrees Fahrenheit. Cook for another hour.

8. Afterwards, allow the turkey and vegetables to rest for 10 minutes before serving. Serve with the vegetables, and enjoy.

Individual Turkey Meatloaves with Green Beans

Serves: 4

Preparation Time: 55 minutes

Ingredients:

- 1 pound ground turkey

- 3 tsp. olive oil

- 1 diced onion

- 1/3 cup barbecue sauce, divided

- 1 cup grated sweet potato

- ½ tsp. pepper

- ½ tsp. salt

- 1 tbsp. maple syrup

- 1 pound of green beans, trimmed

Directions:

1. First, preheat the oven to 400 degrees Fahrenheit.

2. In a large bowl, stir together the turkey, sweet potato, onion, about 3 tbsp. of the barbecue sauce, salt, and the pepper. After fully combining the mixture, create small loaves with your hands. Place the loaves on the pan, and then brush them with the rest of the BBQ sauce.

3. Bake the turkey loaves on the sheet pan for 20 minutes at this time.

4. While the turkey cooks, toss the green beans with the oil and maple syrup. Add salt and pepper. After the turkey comes out of the oven, place the green beans alongside them, and then place the pan back in the oven.

5. Cook the dinner for another 25 minutes, until the meatloaves are completely cooked through.

Mustard-Lathered Salmon with Vegetables

Serves: 4

Preparation Time: 25 minutes

Ingredients:

- 2 cups cherry tomatoes

- 5 cups chopped kale, no ribs or stems

- 2 tbsp. olive oil

- 4 fillets of salmon, about 5 ounces each

- 2 tbsp. chopped parsley

- ½ tsp. salt

- ½ tsp. pepper

Mustard Ingredients:

- 1 tbsp. whole grain mustard

- 3 tbsp. French's sweet mustard

- 1 tbsp. honey

- 1 tbsp. soy sauce

Directions:

1. First, preheat the oven to 400 degrees Fahrenheit.

2. Next, stir together the various mustards in a small bowl, followed by the honey and the soy sauce. Stir well, and set this mixture to the side.

3. Next, place the tomatoes and the kale in a baking sheet. Add the olive oil, salt, and pepper, and toss to coat.

4. Add the salmon over the vegetables, and then brush the salmon with the mustard ingredients.

5. Next, place the baking sheet in the oven, and cook for 18 minutes. At least three times throughout cooking, brush the salmon with the mustard sauce.

6. Afterwards, serve warm with parsley as a garnish.

Delicious Shrimp with Root Vegetables

Serves: 4

Preparation Time: 35 minutes

Ingredients:

- 2 sliced zucchinis

- 1 diced summer squash

- 1 diced red pepper

- 1 cup of halved cherry tomatoes

- 1 diced onion

- ½ tsp. salt

- ½ tsp. pepper

- 3 tbsp. balsamic vinegar, divided

- Juice from one lemon

- ½ tsp. Worcestershire sauce

- 1 ½ pound peeled and deveined shrimp

- 1/8 cup olive oil, plus 1 tbsp., divided

- 1/3 cup chopped basil leaves

Directions:

1. First, preheat the oven to 375 degrees Fahrenheit.

2. Stir together the yellow squash, zucchini, bell pepper, onion, and the tomato on a baking sheet, and add salt, pepper, olive oil, and 2 tbsp. of balsamic vinegar, followed by the juice from one lemon. Stir well, and toss to coat.

3. Next, roast the vegetables for about 25 minutes in the preheated oven.

4. Remove the vegetables from the oven.

5. While you cook the vegetables, add the shrimp to a large bowl, and then add 1 tbsp. olive oil, followed by the last tbsp. of vinegar and the Worcestershire sauce. Toss well to coat.

6. Turn the broiler on at this time. Place the shrimp over the vegetables, and broil the shrimp and vegetables on the highest rack in the oven for five minutes. The shrimp should be cooked all the way through.

7. Add basil over the cooked vegetables and shrimp, and serve warm.

Tilapia with Garlic Green Beans and Tomatoes

Serves: 4

Preparation Time: 50 minutes

Ingredients:

- 4 tomatoes, halved

- 1 tsp. salt

- 1 tsp. pepper

- 10 ounces trimmed green beans

- 1 tbsp. olive oil

- 1/3 cup mayonnaise

- 1 tsp. Dijon mustard

- 2 tsp. lemon juice

- 4 tilapia fillets, about six ounces each

- 1/3 cup breadcrumbs

- 2 tsp. chopped tarragon

- 3 minced garlic cloves

- About eight lemon slices

Directions:

1. First, preheat the oven to 500 degrees Fahrenheit.

2. Slice the tomatoes, and then place them with the cuts up on a baking sheet. Drizzle a bit of olive oil onto the tomatoes, and then salt and pepper them. Bake them in the oven for five minutes.

3. Afterwards, reduce the oven temperature to 450 degrees Fahrenheit.

4. To the side, stir together the salt, garlic, oil, and green beans on a large piece of aluminum foil. Toss the beans to coat them, and then form a packet with the foil. Place the aluminum foil packet on the baking sheet, along with the tomatoes. Bake in the oven for a full 20 minutes at this time.

5. Next, stir together the mayonnaise, tarragon, lemon juice, and the Dijon mustard in a small bowl. Add a bit of salt and pepper, and then spread the mixture over the tilapia fillets. Coat the tilapia with the breadcrumbs.

6. Then, remove the baking sheet from the oven. Push the tomatoes and the packet of beans to the other side of the baking sheet, and then add the tilapia to the free side.

7. Bake the tilapia and vegetables for six minutes at 450 degrees Fahrenheit.

8. After six minutes, turn the broiler to high, without removing the pan from the oven.

9. Broil the fish for three minutes. The breadcrumbs should be golden.

10. Serve the green beans, tomatoes, and tilapia, along with the slices of lemon.

Tuna Nicoise in A Sheet Pan

Serves: 4

Preparation Time: 35 minutes

Ingredients:

- 1 pound of tuna steaks

- 8 tbsp. divided olive oil

- 2 tsp. Herbes de Provence

- 10 ounces green beans, trimmed

- 1 ½ cups cherry tomatoes, halved

- 4 ounces diced potatoes

- ½ cup black olives

- 2 tbsp. white balsamic vinegar

- 1 tsp. maple syrup

- 1 tsp. Dijon mustard

- 4 eggs

- Salt and pepper

- Spinach for serving

Directions:

1. First, preheat the oven to 400 degrees Fahrenheit.

2. Next, place the green beans, potatoes, cherry tomatoes, and black olives on a large baking sheet. Toss the vegetables with two tbsp. of olive oil. Add the Herbes de Provence, and toss well.

3. Next, cook the mixture in the oven for 15 minutes.

4. As the vegetables cook, salt and pepper the tuna steaks. Place the tuna in a baking dish.

5. Next, stir together the vinegar, Dijon mustard, lemon juice, and the maple syrup. As you whisk, add the rest of the olive oil. Salt and pepper to taste.

6. Next, place the eggs in a medium-sized baking sheet. Cover the eggs with water, and place the lid on the baking sheet. Bring the water to a boil on medium heat. Once it begins to boil, remove the baking sheet from the heat. Let it stand, completely covered, for a full eight minutes. This will soft boil the eggs.

7. Next, remove the eggs from the hot water, and rinse them with cold water. Peel when they're cooled to the touch, for the salad.

8. After the vegetables have finished roasting, remove the pan from the oven. Push the vegetables to the side, and place the tuna steaks on the pan. Add about 2 tbsp. of the created vinegar and Dijon mustard dressing to the tuna steaks.

9. Roast for 10 minutes at this time.

10. Afterwards, remove the pan from the oven. Drizzle the rest of the dressing over the tuna and the vegetables, and serve over spinach with the eggs. Enjoy this wonderful salad.

Italian Salmon Sheet Pan Dinner

Serves: 4

Preparation Time: 20 minutes

Ingredients:

- 4 salmon fillets, about 4 ounces each

- 4 minced garlic cloves

- 3 cups sliced fennel

- 3 cups halved Brussels sprouts

- 1 diced onion

- 1/3 cup balsamic vinegar

- 1/3 cup olive oil

- Serve with crumbled feta cheese and chopped parsley

Directions:

1. First, preheat the oven to 425 degrees Fahrenheit.

2. Stir together the garlic, balsamic vinegar, salt, and the olive oil.

3. Next, place the salmon on a baking sheet. Add about half of the balsamic mixture to the salmon, and then toss the vegetables with the rest of the dressing. Arrange the vegetables around the fillets of salmon, and bake the mixture for 15 minutes or until salmon is cooked through.

4. Add feta and parsley to serve, and enjoy.

Asian Fusion Salmon and Broccoli

Serves: 4

Preparation Time: 20 minutes

Ingredients:

- 4 salmon fillets, about 4 ounces each

- 2 tbsp. soy sauce

- 2 tbsp. maple syrup

- 2 tsp. butter

- ½ tsp. salt

- 1 tbsp. rice vinegar

- ¾ pound broccoli

- 2 sliced green onions

Directions:

1. First, preheat the oven to 425 degrees Fahrenheit.

2. To the side, stir together maple syrup, soy sauce, vinegar, butter, and salt in a medium-sized bowl. Coat the salmon in this mixture, and then place the salmon on a baking sheet.

3. Toss the broccoli in the bowl, and add the broccoli around the salmon.

4. Roast the salmon and the broccoli in the preheated oven for 20 minutes or until salmon is cooked through. The salmon should be flakey.

5. Top the salmon and the broccoli with the green onions, and enjoy.

Parmesan Tilapia

Serves: 4

Preparation Time: 20 minutes

Ingredients:

- 1 cup grated Parmesan
- 1 tbsp. chopped parsley
- 2 tsp. paprika
- 4 fillets of tilapia
- 1 tsp. salt
- 1 tsp. pepper
- Olive oil

Directions:

1. First, preheat the oven to 400 degrees Fahrenheit.

2. Next, stir together the paprika, Parmesan, salt, parsley, and pepper in a small bowl.

3. Next, drizzle olive oil over the tilapia, and then press the tilapia into the Parmesan mixture.

4. Place the tilapia on a baking sheet, and bake the tilapia for 12 minutes.

Sheet Pan Vegetables and Steak

Serves: 8

Preparation Time: 20 minutes

Fresh Herb Butter Ingredients:

- 1 tbsp. chopped basil

- 1 tbsp. chopped thyme

- 1 tbsp. chopped rosemary

- 5 tbsp. butter, unsalted and softened

- ½ tsp. salt

- ½ tsp. pepper

Steak and Vegetable Ingredients:

- 2 pounds sirloin steak, about 1-inch thick

- 1 pound of carrots, chopped

- 1 pound asparagus, chopped

- 2 tbsp. olive oil

- 2 ½ cups cherry tomatoes

- 1 tsp. thyme, dried

- 3 minced garlic cloves

- ½ tsp. salt

- ½ tsp. pepper

Directions:

1. First, place a baking rack about six inches beneath the broiler. Pre-heat the broiler.

2. Next, stir together the chopped basil, thyme, rosemary, unsalted butter, salt, and pepper. Set this mixture to the side.

3. Next, place the carrots, tomatoes, and asparagus on a baking sheet. Add garlic, olive oil, and thyme to the baking sheet, before seasoning with salt and pepper and tossing the ingredients well to coat.

4. Next, place the baking sheet in the oven, and broil for about eight minutes. The carrots should be slightly tender.

5. Next, salt and pepper the steaks. Add them to the baking sheet in a single layer, and then place the baking sheet back in the oven. Broil for three minutes.

6. Then, remove the pan, flip the steaks, and broil them for an additional three minutes. Adjust time to cook the steaks if you like them more 'well done'.

7. Serve the steak and vegetables with the herb butter overtop, and enjoy.

Quick and Delicious Salisbury Steak

Serves: 2

Preparation Time: 35 minutes

Ingredients:

- 8 ounces ground beef, lean

- 1 onion, diced

- 1 tbsp. olive oil

- 1 tsp. onion powder

- 1 tsp. dry mustard

- 1 tbsp. Worcestershire sauce

- 1 tsp. garlic powder

- 1 tsp. salt

- 1 tsp. pepper

Directions:

1. First, preheat the oven to 400 degrees Fahrenheit.

2. Slice the onion from the tip to the roof, and then place the flat side of the onion upon the baking sheet. Toss the onions with the olive oil.

3. Next, to the side, stir together the ground beef, Worcestershire sauce, mustard powder, garlic powder, onion powder, and a bit of salt and pepper. Mix with your hands, ensuring you don't over mix, as the meat won't stick together after too much handling.

4. Form two patties with your hands, and place the steaks in the baking pan, alongside the onions.

5. Bake the steaks for 30 minutes, and serve warm.

Baked Tofu with Citrus Splash

Serves: 4

Preparation Time: 40 minutes

Ingredients:

- 1 cup chopped cilantro, divided

- 1/3 cup minced garlic

- 1 cup lime juice

- 4 tsp. ground cumin, divided

- 1 tsp. paprika, divided

- ½ tsp. salt

- ½ tsp. pepper

- 1 pound medium tofu, sliced into ½-inch pieces

- 1 diced onion

- ½ tbsp. honey

- 3 red peppers, sliced

Directions:

1. First, preheat the oven to 450 degrees Fahrenheit.

2. Next, stir together about half the cilantro, lime juice, garlic, half of the cumin, and half of the paprika together in a small bowl.

3. Next, add salt and pepper to the mixture, and pour half cup of this marinade into a plastic bag. Add the sliced tofu to the bag, and shake it well. Allow the tofu to marinate for 15 minutes.

4. Add the leftover marinade, cilantro, oil, honey, and all remaining spices to a blender. Blend well until smooth and then season it with salt and pepper.

5. To the side, stir together the onion and red pepper, and toss with salt and pepper.

6. Drain the tofu, and season with salt and pepper. Place the tofu on one side of a baking sheet. Add the vegetables on the other side.

7. Roast the dinner in the preheated oven for 25 minutes. Afterwards, divide the tofu and the vegetables on your plates for serving, and pour the sauce over the tofu and vegetables. Add any extra cilantro to taste, and enjoy.

Stuffed with goat cheese

Serves: 4

Preparation Time: 5 hours 30 minutes

Ingredients:

- ¼ cup of red wine

- ¼ cup of balsamic vinegar

- 2 tablespoon of Dijon mustard

- 2 tablespoon of soy sauce

- 1 cup of extra virgin olive oil

- 4 cloves of garlic, peeled and thinly sliced

- 1 tablespoon of salt Dash of black pepper

- 1, 2 to 3 pounds of flank steak

Ingredients for the stuffing:

- ½ cup of pancetta, cooked and chopped

- 8 ounces of goat cheese

- 3 cups of spinach, drained and excess liquid drained

Directions:

1. Use a large bowl and add in the red wine, vinegar, mustard, soy sauce, olive oil, garlic and dash of salt and black pepper. Whisk until mixed.

2. Add in the flank steak and cover. Set in the fridge to marinate for 4 hours.

3. Place a large baking sheet over low heat. Chop the pancetta and place into the baking sheet. Cook for 20 to 30 minutes. Drain the excess fat and set the pancetta aside.

4. Add the spinach into the baking sheet and cook for 1 to 2 minutes or until fragrant. Remove from the pan and squeeze out the excess liquid. Add into a bowl with the pancetta and goat cheese. Stir well to mix.

5. Remove the flank steak from the marinade and place onto a flat surface. Beat with a meat mallet until ¼ inch in thickness.

6. Spread the stuffing onto the flank steak. Roll and tie with twine to seal. Season with a dash of salt and black pepper.

7. Heat up the oven to 400 degrees.

8. Place the rolled flank steak onto a large baking sheet and drizzle a few drops of olive oil over the top.

9. Place into the oven to bake for 15 to 25 minutes or until cooked through. Remove and allow to rest for 15 minutes before serving.

Ratatouille with Goat Cheese

Serves: 8

Preparation Time: 45 minutes

Ingredients:

- 12 ounces of tomato puree

- 4 minced garlic cloves

- 1 diced onion

- 2 tbsp. butter, cut into small pieces

- 1 diced red pepper

- 1 diced eggplant

- 1 diced zucchini

- 3 diced squash

- 2 tbsp. olive oil

- 6 ounces goat's cheese

- 1 tbsp. chopped basil

- 1 tsp. salt

- 1 tsp. pepper

Directions:

1. First, preheat the oven to 375 degrees Fahrenheit.

2. Add tomato puree to a sheet pan, spreading it around. Next, add the onion, garlic, and a bit of salt and pepper. Stir well.

3. Add the butter pieces to the top of this mixture.

4. Arrange the remaining vegetables around the pan evenly, and then drizzle the olive oil over the vegetables. Sprinkle a bit more salt and pepper over the top.

5. Place the ratatouille in the oven and bake for 40 minutes, or until the vegetables are tender.

6. Remove the pan at this time, and turn on the broiler.

7. Crumble the goat cheese over the vegetables, and broil the ratatouille in the broiler for one minute, or until the goat cheese melts.

8. Add the chopped basil over the vegetables, and serve warm.

Mexican Kale Sheet Pan

Serves: 15

Preparation Time: 20 minutes

Ingredients:

- 4 cups kale, frozen

- 1 cup frozen corn

- 15 ounces black beans, from a can, drained

- 1 cup chopped red peppers

- 1 tbsp. olive oil

- ¼ tsp. paprika

- ¼ tsp. cumin

- ½ tsp. salt

- ½ avocado

Dressing Ingredients:

- ½ avocado

- ½ cup cilantro, chopped

- Juice from ½ lime

- ¼ cup water

- 2 tbsp. yogurt, plain

- ½ tsp. chili powder

- ½ tsp. salt

- ½ tsp. cumin

Directions:

1. First, preheat the oven to 400 degrees Fahrenheit.

2. Next, stir together the black beans, kale, corn, and the peppers on a baking sheet. Add the olive oil overtop, along with the spices and salt. Stir well.

3. Next, bake the mixture in the preheated oven for 15 minutes. Afterwards, remove the pan from the oven.

4. As the vegetables cook, make the dressing. Place the half avocado, cilantro, lime juice, yogurt, chili powder, salt, and cumin in a food processor, and pulse for 20 seconds. Afterwards, pour the dressing into a small bowl.

5. Serve the vegetables, topped with avocado and the dressing, and enjoy.

Simple Salisbury Steak

Serves: 8

Preparation Time: 20 minutes

Ingredients for the steak:

- 3 pounds of beef, lean and ground

- ½ cup of panko breadcrumbs

- 2 eggs, large

- 2 tablespoon of ketchup, low in sugar

- 4 tablespoon of mustard, dried

- 8 dashes of Worcestershire sauce

- 1 tablespoon of salt

- 1 tablespoon of black pepper

- 1 tablespoon of garlic, powdered

- 1 tablespoon of onion, powdered

- 2 tablespoon of butter

- 2 tablespoon of extra virgin olive oil

Ingredients for the gravy:

- 1 onion, sliced thinly

- 4 cups of beef broth

- 2 tablespoon of ketchup, low in sugar

- 2 tablespoon of kitchen bouquet

- 8 dashes of Worcestershire sauce

- 2 tablespoon of cornstarch

Directions:

1. Use a large bowl and add in all of the ingredients for the steak except for the butter and extra virgin olive oil. Stir well to mix and form this mixture into patties.

2. Place a large baking sheet over medium heat. Add in the extra virgin olive oil and butter. As soon as the butter melts add in the beef patties. Cook for 8 minutes on each side or until cooked through.

3. Remove the cooked patties from the baking sheet and transfer to a large plate.

4. Add the sliced onions into the baking sheet. Cook for 5 to 10 minutes or until soft.

5. Then add in the beef broth, low sugar ketchup, kitchen bouquet and Worcestershire sauce. Whisk until smooth in consistency.

6. Add in the cornstarch and whisk to mix. Continue to cook for an additional 2 minutes or until thick in consistency.

7. Add the cooked patties into the gravy and toss to mix.

8. Remove from heat and serve.

Lemon-ed Broccoli Florets

Serves: 4

Preparation Time: 15 minutes

Ingredients:

- 4 cups broccoli florets

- ½ tsp. crushed red pepper

- Olive oil

- 1 lemon, sliced in half and zested

- ½ tsp. salt

- ½ tsp. pepper

Directions:

1. First, preheat the oven to 400 degrees Fahrenheit.

2. Next, place the broccoli on a baking sheet. Add a bit of olive oil, and then toss with the lemon zest and the red pepper flakes.

3. Season the broccoli with salt and pepper.

4. Next, roast the broccoli for 12 minutes. Finish off the broccoli with some lemon juice, and toss to coast.

Sheet Pan Eggs with Asparagus

Serves: 6

Preparation Time: 10 minutes

Ingredients:

- 12 eggs

- ½ tsp. salt

- ½ tsp. pepper

- 1 cup shaved asparagus

Directions:

1. Preheat the oven to 350 degrees Fahrenheit.

2. Crack the eggs directly into the sheet pan, and swirl them around, cracking the yolks.

3. Spread out the asparagus evenly, and then salt and pepper the mixture well.

4. Next, bake the mixture for 10 minutes, or until the egg is hard and spongy.

5. Slice the baked egg mixture into pieces, and enjoy.

Low Carb Vegetable Lasagna

Serves: 8

Preparation Time: 90 minutes

Ingredients:

- 2 zucchini, large
- 1 diced onion
- 1/3 cup red wine
- 1 tbsp. olive oil
- 16 ounces tomato sauce
- 1 tbsp. chopped oregano
- 3 tbsp. chopped basil
- 1 egg
- 1 cup tomato paste
- 2 tsp. black pepper
- 1 diced green pepper
- 2 tbsp. chopped parsley
- 16 ounces thawed spinach, if once frozen
- 1 sliced pound of mushrooms
- 10 ounces mozzarella cheese
- 10 ounces Parmesan cheese
- 15 ounces ricotta cheese

Directions:

1. First, preheat the oven to 325 degrees Fahrenheit.

2. Next, slice the zucchini length-wise, into thin, noodle slices. Sprinkle the zoodles with salt, and place them to the side to dry over paper towels.

3. Next, sauté the onion and green pepper in a large baking sheet in the olive oil for five minutes. Add the tomato sauce and paste, along with the wine, oregano, and basil. Stir well, adding water if the sauce is too thick. Bring the mixture to a boil. Once it begins to boil, simmer the mixture for 20 minutes, stirring all the time.

4. To the side, stir together the ricotta, egg, and parsley in a medium-sized bowl.

5. Next, assemble the lasagna. Place the vegetable mixture at the bottom of a pan, followed by half of the zucchini noodles. Then, add half of the ricotta mixture, followed by all of the mushrooms, followed by all of the spinach. Then, add half the mozzarella cheese.

6. Repeat layering at this time, followed by Parmesan cheese.

7. Cover the lasagna with foil, and then bake the lasagna for 45 minutes.

8. After 45 minutes, remove the foil. Increase the oven's temperature to 350 degrees Fahrenheit, and bake for another 15 minutes.

9. Allow the lasagna to sit for 10 minutes, and then serve warm. Enjoy.

Roasted Pineapple with Pistachios

Serves: 4

Preparation Time: 30 minutes

Ingredients:

- 2 tbsp. honey

- 1 ½ cups pineapple, sliced into wedges or cubes

- 1/3 cup crème fraiche

- 1/3 cup pistachios, chopped

- 2 tbsp. fresh mint leaves, chopped

Directions:

1. First, preheat the oven to 450 degrees Fahrenheit.

2. Add the pineapple to a large bowl, and then add the honey. Toss it to coat.

3. Then, place the pineapple on a baking sheet. Roast the pineapple in the oven for 15 minutes.

4. After 15 minutes, flip the pineapple, and then roast for another 15 minutes. Allow it to cool.

5. Divide up the pineapple, and serve with the pistachios and the crème fraiche.

Apricot Tarts

Serves: 12

Preparation Time: 35 minutes

Ingredients:

- 1 14-ounce package of frozen puff pastry, thawed

- ¾ pound apricots, sliced into wedges

- Ground black pepper

- ½ tbsp. honey

- Sea salt

Directions:

1. First, preheat your oven to 425 degrees Fahrenheit.

2. Slice the puff pastry into 4-inch squares, and then place the pastries on a baking sheet. Prick at the pastries with a fork. Then, top the pastries with the apricots, leaving a slight border at the edges. Season with black pepper.

3. At this time, bake the tarts for 30 minutes, rotating them after about 15 minutes, until they're golden brown on the edges. Add sea salt, and serve.

No Grain Chocolate Sheet Cake

Serves: 20

Preparation Time: 40 minutes

Ingredients:

- 2 cups almond flour

- 1 cup Swerve Sweetener

- 1 tbsp. baking powder

- 1/3 cup whey protein powder, unflavored

- 1/3 cup coconut flour

- 3 eggs

- 1/3 cup cocoa powder

- 3 eggs

- ½ cup butter

- ½ tsp. salt

- 1/3 cup heavy cream

- 1/3 cup water

- 1 tsp. vanilla

Frosting Ingredients:

- ½ cup butter

- 1 ½ cups powdered Swerve Sweetener

- 1/3 cup cocoa powder

- 1/3 cup cream

- 1/3 cup water

- ¼ tsp. xanthan gum

- 1 cup diced pecans

Directions:

1. First, preheat oven to 325 degrees Fahrenheit.

2. Next, in a large bowl, stir together the sweetener, almond flour, coconut flour, baking powder, protein powder, and salt.

3. Next, add the butter, cocoa powder, and the water to a baking sheet and melt over medium heat, stirring all the time. Bring the mixture to a boil, then remove the baking sheet from the heat. Add the mixture to the flour bowl, and stir well.

4. Add the vanilla, eggs, and cream to the bowl, and stir well until completely combined.

5. Pour the mixture into a baking pan, and allow it to bake for 20 minutes. The cake should be set in the center.

6. Next, make the frosting. Stir together the cocoa powder, butter, cream, and water in a medium-sized baking sheet, and bring the mixture to a simmer. Stir well until smooth.

7. Add the vanilla to the mixture, followed by the powdered sweetener. Stir well. After fully combined, add the xanthan gum. Stir.

8. Next, pour the frosting over the cake, and sprinkle the cake with pecans. Allow the sheet cake to cool until the frosting sets. This should take about one hour.

Cheese Blintz with Blueberries

Serves: 1

Preparation Time: 13 minutes

Ingredients

- 1 medium egg

- 1 tablespoon half & half

- 1 scoop protein shake powder, vanilla

- 1 pat of butter

- 1 tablespoon of olive oil

- 2 tablespoon ricotta cheese

- 1 tablespoon Greek yogurt, plain

- 1 packet sweetener

- 1 tablespoon cinnamon

- ½ cup blueberries

Directions

1. Combine the ricotta cheese, Greek yogurt, sweetener and cinnamon in a bowl, mix well.

2. Combine the egg, protein powder, and cream. Whisk until all lumps are dissolved, and the mixture is well-blended.

3. Coat a non-stick baking sheet with the olive oil.

4. At medium heat, melt butter in the baking sheet and pour the batter on top.

5. Swirl the baking sheet until the batter is evenly distributed. When the batter has set, gently turn the blintz to the other side.

6. Let cook for one minute until the batter is set, but not browned.

7. Gently fold half the blueberries into the filling.

8. Place the filling in the middle of the blitz.

9. Roll into a pancake and serve with the remaining blueberries.

10. Mix the filling and place in the fridge in a covered container. Place the blueberries in a zip-lock bag and place in the freezer.

No Bake Cheesecake

Serves: 12

Preparation Time: 6 hours 15 minutes

Ingredients:

- ½ cup of almond flour

- ¼ cup of butter, melted

- 16 ounces of cream cheese, soft

- ¾ cup of artificial sweetener

- ½ tablespoon of pure vanilla

- ½ tablespoon of lemon juice, fresh

- ½ tablespoon of salt

Directions:

1. Spray a baking sheet with cooking spray and line with paper muffin lines.

2. Use a large bowl and add in the almond flour and butter. Stir well until mixed. Pour this mixture into the bottom of each muffin cup. Press flat to make a crust.

3. Use a separate bowl and add in the cream cheese, artificial sweetener, pure vanilla, fresh lemon juice and dash of salt. Beat with an electric mixer until creamy in consistency. Pour this mixture over the crusts.

4. Place the baking sheet into the freezer to freeze for 2 hours.

5. Remove after this time and transfer into the fridge to thaw for 3 to 4 hours. Serve. Flank Steak Stuffed with Pancetta and Goat Cheese This is a great tasting keto friendly dish you can make for lunch or dinner.

Seven Layer Salad

Serves: 10

Preparation Time: 23 minutes

Ingredients

- 4 cups shredded butter lettuce

- 4 cups shredded romaine lettuce

- 1 cup peas

- 1 cup diced bell peppers, red and yellow

- 1 cup grape tomatoes, halved

- 1 cup sliced celery

- ½ cup red onion

- ¾ cup Greek yogurt

- ¾ cup mayonnaise

- 3 hard-boiled eggs

- 2 teaspoons cider vinegar

- 1 packet Splenda

- ¼ teaspoon garlic salt

- ½ cup pepper-jack cheese, hand-shredded

- 3 strips cooked bacon, crumbled

Directions

1. Using a large glass baking sheet, 9x13 sized, layer the two lettuces.

2. Layer the peas, then the peppers, then the tomatoes, celery and onion. —

3. Place the diced eggs next.

4. Combine the dressing ingredients: yogurt, mayonnaise, vinegar, garlic salt, Splenda, and a dash of black pepper.

5. Spread the dressing over the salad.

6. Garnish with the pepper-jack cheese and bacon.

7. Place in one cup containers. Close with a lid and refrigerate.

Parmesan Halibut

Serves: 6

Preparation Time: 18 minutes

Ingredients:

- 6 halibut fillets

- 1 stick of butter, soft

- 3 tablespoon of parmesan cheese, grated

- 1 tablespoon of panko breadcrumbs, dried

- 1 tablespoon of salt

- ½ tablespoon of black pepper

- 2 tablespoon of garlic, powdered 1 tablespoon of parsley, dried

Directions:

1. Preheat the oven to 400 degrees.

2. Add all of the ingredients except for the halibut into a large bowl. Stir well to mix.

3. Pat the halibut fillets dry with a few paper towels and place onto a large baking sheet.

4. Cover each halibut fillet with the parmesan butter mixture.

5. Place into the oven to bake for 10 to 12 minutes.

6. After this time preheat the broiler to high. Broil for 2 to 3 minutes or until golden brown.

7. Remove and serve immediately.

Pork Chops with Fennel Crust

Serves: 4

Preparation Time: 50 minutes

Ingredients:

- 1 ¼ pounds pork loin chops

- 3 minced garlic cloves

- 2 tbsp. fennel seeds

- 1 tsp. paprika

- 2 tbsp. olive oil, divided

- 2 sliced shallots

- ½ cup chopped parsley

- 2 tsp. red wine vinegar

Directions:

1. First, preheat the oven to 450 degrees Fahrenheit. Place the fennel seeds on a baking sheet, and toast them over medium-high heat, tossing them. Cook them for four minutes, or until fragrant. Now, allow them to cool.

2. Next, stir together the fennel seeds, paprika, garlic, and one tbsp. of olive oil in a small bowl.

3. To the side, salt and pepper the pork, and then place the pork in a large plastic bag. Add the fennel seed mixture, seal the bag, and turn it, coating the pork completely. Allow the pork to marinate for 30 minutes.

4. Next, heat the last tbsp. of olive oil in a baking sheet over medium-high. Place the pork chops in the baking sheet and cook for about four minutes on each side, adding the shallots to the pan when you flip.

5. Afterwards, place the pork chops on a baking pan, and roast for an additional 15 minutes in the preheated oven.

6. Remove the pan from the oven, and add the vinegar and parsley to the pork chops, stirring well.

7. Cut the meat from the bone, and slice the pork against the grain. Serve the pork with shallots and pan juices, and enjoy.

Asian Spiced Pork Chops

Serves: 4

Preparation Time: 4 hours marinade, plus 25 minutes

Ingredients:

- 4 pork chops, without bones and trimmed of fat
- 2 tbsp. maple syrup
- 2 tbsp. olive oil
- 1 tsp. Chinese five spice powder
- 1/3 cup soy sauce
- 2 tbsp. rice vinegar
- 1 tsp. sesame oil, toasted
- 2-inch piece of ginger, grated
- 2 cups broccoli florets
- 1 chopped pineapple
- 1 tsp. sea salt
- 1 tsp. pepper

Directions:

1. In a medium-sized bowl, stir together the olive oil, maple syrup, vinegar, soy sauce, five spice powder, ginger, and the sesame oil.

2. Next, place the pork chops in a sealable bag, and add the marinade. Allow the pork to rest in the marinade in the refrigerator for about four hours or overnight, if possible. Make sure that you turn the pork every few hours to marinate evenly.

3. Preheat your oven to 425 degrees Fahrenheit.

4. Place the pork chops on a sheet pan, spaced out.

5. To the side, stir together the broccoli florets and the pineapple. Add about half of the remaining marinade from the baggie, and toss the ingredients well to coat. Place the broccoli and the pineapple on the pan, and then arrange them evenly.

6. Afterwards, bake the pork and vegetables for 20 minutes, until the pork chops are cooked completely through. Serve immediately, and enjoy.

Pork Saltimbocca with Onions

Serves: 4

Preparation Time: 40 minutes

Ingredients:

- 4 slices of pork, about 6 ounces each

- 4 sliced onions

- 2 sliced red peppers

- 1 cup white wine

- 3 tbsp. olive oil, divided

- Salt and pepper

- 1/3 cup sage, chopped

- 8 slices prosciutto, sliced thin

Directions:

1. First, preheat the oven to 450 degrees Fahrenheit.

2. Next, pierce at the pork slices with a paring knife, and place the pork in a single layer in a baking dish. Add the wine to the baking dish, and allow the pork to marinate for the next steps.

3. Next, place the sliced onions and peppers in a medium-sized bow. Add one tablespoon of olive oil, and then salt and pepper the onion. Toss the onion and peppers to coat, but do it lightly, so that you don't break up the onions too much.

4. Next, place the onions and peppers on a baking sheet, spreading them in a single layer. Sprinkle on the remaining oil, and sage, and then roast them in the preheated oven for 15 minutes.

5. At this time, remove the pork from the white wine, and pat it dry. Salt and pepper it well, and then place prosciutto on top of the

pork slices. Place the pork over the onions and peppers, and roast the pork for 11 minutes, or until a thermometer inserted into the center reads 135 degrees Fahrenheit.

6. Allow the pork to rest for about 10 minutes, and then serve warm. Enjoy.

Eastern Seaboard Stuffed Cabbage Rolls

Serves: 4

Preparation Time: 70 minutes

Ingredients:

- 1 pound ground beef

- 2 tbsp. olive oil

- 1 tsp. sesame oil

- 4 minced garlic cloves

- 3 minced tbsp. ginger

- 1 shredded carrot

- 1 cup cooked cauliflower, riced with a fork

- 1 tbsp. soy sauce

- 3 chopped scallions

- 5 ounces sliced mushrooms

- 1/3 cup chopped cilantro

- 1 tbsp. rice wine vinegar

- 1 head of cabbage, with the leaves separated

- 1/3 cup hoisin sauce

- 2 tbsp. water

Directions:

1. First, prepare your cauliflower. Boil it until tender, and then drain it, squeezing out as much water as you can. Rice it with your fork. This is low-carbohydrate rice, for your cabbage rolls.

2. Preheat the oven to 375 degrees Fahrenheit.

3. Next, add the olive oil and the sesame oil to a medium-sized pan, and add the garlic, ginger, and mushrooms. Sauté them for about six minutes. The mushrooms should begin to brown.

4. To the side, in a large bowl, stir together the ground beef, shredded carrot, riced cauliflower, soy sauce, scallions, and the rice wine vinegar. Use your hands to combine the ingredients together until well mixed. Add the olive oil and sesame oil to the beef and carrot mixture, and continue to stir with your hands.

5. Next, lay out the cabbage leaves on a baking sheet. Place about a half cup of the filling into the stem-end of the cabbage leaf, and roll the leaf ends, folding in the sides to make it a closed pocket. Continue until you have no mixture left.

6. Place the cabbage leaves seams downward on the baking sheet.

7. To the side, stir together the water and the hoisin sauce, and then brush the sauce over the cabbage rolls.

8. Bake the cabbage rolls in the preheated oven for a full 30 minutes. Remove the baking dish from the oven, and allow them to cool for about five minutes.

Conclusion

The Low Carb Sheet Pan Dinners book is an extensive, one-stop-shop for all of your sheet pan dinner needs, allowing you to cook nutritious, wholesome, and delicious meals quickly, without copious pots and pans. With a low-carb dinner plan in hand, and recipes containing just 15 grams of carbohydrates per serving or fewer, you can rev your body's metabolism, amp your muscles, lose fat quickly, and remain satisfied, without the hunger pangs that come with other diet plans. And you can do that any night of the week, without hassle, and without sacrificing flavor.

The chicken, seafood, turkey, beef, pork, vegetarian, or dessert recipes in this book offer nutritional information, including protein count, fat count, net carbohydrate count, and calories, allowing you to keep close track of your dietary needs, without going over on your requirements and ultimately gaining weight. And when you have a million things going on in your life—whether they're school-related, family-related, or just Netflix cue-related—you're going to need the time you save using just a single sheet pan, with many recipes allowing you to stir the ingredients directly in the pan and then bake in 30 minutes or less.

Good luck with your low carb diet lifestyle. You deserve to be the healthiest person you can possibly be, with plenty of time to spare in your otherwise harried existence. Enjoy!

Made in the USA
Middletown, DE
27 August 2019